Jazz Style and Technique
Workbook for all Saxophones
By: Brian J. Kane

For additional materials, articles, exercises, songs, and other titles, please visit us at www.jazzpath.com

ISBN 0-9760977-1-0

PO Box 381810
Cambridge MA 02238
www.jazzpath.com

Cover Design By:
Elise Deflaminis

Sight Reading Continuum©

Level 6

Accurate sight reading in compositions that reflect extreme chromaticism while in key signatures of more than 4 sharps or 4 flats. Musician shows accuracy with advanced syncopations and long technical phrases. All previous rules for dynamics, vibrato, and inflections are habitually followed.

Level 5

Accurate sight reading in compositions that reflect chromaticism rather than diatonic playing while in key signatures of up to 4 sharps and 4 flats. Student accurately reads complicated syncopations and all "4" and "6" time signature variations. All previous rules for dynamics, vibrato, and inflections are habitually followed.

Level 4

Accurate sight reading in compositions that reflect all major key signatures. Chromaticism is common in key signatures of up to 3 sharps and 3 flats. Student accurately reads phrases with syncopations and sixteenth notes. All previous rules for dynamics, vibrato, and inflections are habitually followed without the need for notation.

Level 3

Accurate sight reading in compositions with key signatures of up to 3 sharps and 3 flats. Rhythms include syncopations and sixteenth notes. Chromaticism is introduced. Student observes all breath, articulation, and dynamic markings. Vibrato is habitually added in appropriate places. Style inflections are added when notated.

Use this book in conjunction with the JazzPath book "Creative Jazz Sight Reading" and move all the way from Level 1 to Level 3!

Level 2

Accurate sight reading in compositions with key signatures of up to 2 sharps and 2 flats. Rhythms include syncopations and sixteenth notes. Occasional chromatic notes are allowed. Student observes all breath, articulation, and dynamic markings. Student plays vibrato when reminded by notation.

Level 1

Accurate sight reading in compositions with key signatures of up to 2 sharps and 2 flats. Rhythms include quarter notes and quarter rests and eighth notes and eighth rests. Student observes most breath, articulation, and dynamic markings. Student plays vibrato when reminded by notation.

jazz path
MUSIC PUBLISHING®

PO Box 381810 Cambridge, MA 02238
www.jazzpath.com

Jazz Style and Technique
Workbook for all Saxophones
By: Brian J. Kane

CONTENTS

INTRODUCTION

This workbook has three main objectives. The first is to offer instruction on how to correctly interpret and apply swing articulations in jazz. Proper articulations are essential in order to sound authentic in jazz. Understanding and applying the articulation rules in this workbook will improve the authenticity and execution of your playing and will help make you a more competent jazz stylist.

The second objective of this book is to improve technique by learning the same melody in several different keys. Exploring new keys within the context of a melody that is familiar has two main benefits. First, it allows you to focus solely on playing the correct notes because the rhythms are already familiar, and second, it forces you to use your ear to correct mistakes. Using this process, you should gain a certain amount of fluency within the key signatures offered in this workbook.

The third objective of this book is to instruct in the use of basic jazz inflections. Jazz inflections are note ornaments or alterations that add color and personal expression to phrases. Making the use of jazz inflections a habit is always a large hurdle for inexperienced musicians. This workbook offers consistent opportunities to add practical and stylistically appropriate jazz inflections.

How to Use this Workbook

This book consists of a description of swing articulations and jazz inflections, followed by 15 short compositions. Each composition is designed to explore different aspects of swing articulation. Each composition is written in three different key signatures to help you gain technical fluency on your instrument and is further expanded at the back of the book with proper jazz inflections notated.

Play each composition in the easiest key signatures first! Focus on playing the proper articulations and adding simple inflections. When instructed to, turn to the back of the workbook and play the compositions with the inflections that are given. Once you've mastered adding inflections in an easy key, move on to some of the harder key signatures. While you're practicing the harder key signatures, make sure you remain focused on proper articulations and try to add in your own inflections. Here are some tips for new key signatures.

1. Make sure you know the major scale that corresponds to the key signature! Memorize it. Play it on your instrument evenly, accurately, and quickly. Play the scale ascending, descending, and any other way you can think of!

2. Always write in ALL the accidentals when you're learning a new key signature. Write in all the accidentals in each new song you learn.

3. Make sure you understand and can play all of the rhythms in a song BEFORE you start focusing on the notes. Write in the countings for all of the rhythms in each song. Play all of the rhythms in each song on one note. Practice humming the rhythms. Practice humming the melody while you finger the notes on your instrument. Then try playing the composition.

4. If you've practiced hard and still can't play a composition, YOU HAVEN'T FOLLOWED STEPS 1-3!

Good luck! I hope you have fun working through this book and I hope this gives you a better understanding of swing articulations and jazz inflections.

                                              -Brian Kane

Swing Eighth Notes

In a swing feel, eighth notes are not even. Eighth notes on down beats have a slightly longer rhythmic value than those on upbeats. It is this difference in rhythmic value that gives eighth notes their "swing" feel. Play the following exercise.

Play this exercise at a very fast tempo. Imagine that each of these is a very slow eighth note!

This is how eighth notes sound if you play them very slowly. The first note has more rhythmic value than the second!

The next step is to make sure you can play triplets. Triplets are the rhythmic foundation for swing eighth notes. Play, count, and say the following exercise.

Once you're really comfortable playing triplets, we're going to add some ties. When notes are tied together you must hold them out for their combined rhythmic value. The first part of the triplet has more rhythmic value than the second.

This is how swing eighth notes sound!

PLAY THIS G MAJOR SCALE AND SWING THE EIGHTH NOTES.

IF YOU ARE SWINGING THE EIGHTH NOTES CORRECTLY IT SHOULD SOUND LIKE THIS.

NOW TRY PLAYING ALL THE SCALES YOU KNOW IN SWING EIGHTH NOTES!

TEMPO MATTERS WHEN PLAYING SWING EIGHT NOTES. ALL OF THE EXAMPLES THAT

I HAVE WRITTEN ARE MEANT TO BE PLAYED A MODERATE SWING TEMPO. THE SLOWER THE TEMPO, THE MORE EXAGERRATED THE SWING FEEL. IN A SLOW TEMPO MORE RHYTHMIC VALUE IS PLACED ON THE FIRST OF THE TWO EIGHTH NOTES. THE FASTER THE TEMPO, THE THE LESS EXAGERRATED THE SWING FEEL. IN A FAST TEMPO EIGHTH NOTES RECIEVE VIRTUALLY EQUAL RHTYHMIC VALUE.

EVERY EXCERCISE IN THIS WORKBOOK USES SWING EIGHTH NOTES. MAKE SWING EIGHTH NOTES A HABITUAL PART OF YOUR PLAYING!

Swing Articulations

The term "articulation" refers to way that people who play wind instruments tongue different notes. Swing articulations are virtually never written into songs. The expectation is that the musician will correctly interpret the phrase with typical swing articulations. Most musicians learn these articulations through listening to jazz and copying established jazz musicians. Though emulating other musicians is incredibly beneficial, it is not the only way to learn swing articulations.

Throughout this workbook I will use only two articulations: long and short. In musical terminology, long is referred to as "legato" and short is referred to as "staccato". There are several ways that composers notate legato and staccato articulations in music. Throughout this workbook, I will notate legato articulations with a dash over or under the note unless there are slur markings between two eighth notes. Where there are slur markings, tongue the first note "doo" and slur to the second. I will notate staccato articulations with a dot over or under the note. It might look like this:

I prefer to articulate with syllables that start with a "d" sound. Some people prefer to use syllables with a "t" sound. Both ways work. You should decide which syllable you are comfortable with and like the best. Feel free to substitute "t" syllables throughout this workbook.

The Four Rules of Swing Articulation

I have found that learning the "rules" of swing articulations and reinforcing the "rules" through compositions has dramatically helped my students improve their jazz style. These rules apply virtually all of the time. Practice them. If you make them a habit you will drastically improve your style.

RULE 1: Any eighth note that is followed by any type of rest is always SHORT! Repeated eighth notes on the same pitch are always legato.

Say "Doo-Doo-Doo-Doot"

RULE 2: When articulating triplets, tongue the first note of the triplet legato, slur to the second, and tongue the last note staccato. You should say "Doo-Ooh-Doot." When a triplet occurs on a repeated note, tongue the first two notes of the triplet legato and the last staccato. You should say "Doo-Doo-Doot."

Say "Doo-Doo-Doot"   Say "Doo-Ooh-Doot"

RULE 3:

WHEN PLAYING A SERIES OF EIGHTH NOTES THAT START ON THE DOWN BEAT, TONGUE THE FIRST AND SECOND LEGATO, THEN TONGUE EVERY OTHER OFF BEAT LEGATO. SAY "DOO-DOO-OOH-DOO-OOH-DOO," ETC.

SAY "DOO-DOO-OOH-DOO-OOH-DOO"

RULE 4:

WHEN PLAYING A SERIES OF EIGHTH NOTES THAT START ON AN UPBEAT, TONGUE THE FIRST LEGATO AND THEN TONGUE EVERY OTHER OFF BEAT LEGATO.

SAY "DOO-OOH-DOO-OOH-DOO-OOH-DOOT"

IT IS CRUCIAL TO MAKE JAZZ ARTICULATIONS A HABIT! DO THEM ALL THE TIME, EVEN WHEN THEY ARE NOT WRITTEN IN.

Jazz Inflections

The use of inflections is a critical element of playing in a jazz style. Jazz musicians use inflections constantly to add color and feel to their playing. Unfortunately, these inflections are rarely written into music. There are few rules for the use of inflections. Inflections are played when the artist chooses to play them.

Instrumentalists must get in the habit of using inflections to improve their style. The only way to create this type of habit is through practice and repetition. When using this workbook, first play each composition with the correct rhythm, notes, and articulations. Once the composition is mechanically correct, add inflections.

This workbook will only use three of the dozens of possible inflections. It is useful to master a few common inflections and make a habit of constantly using them. The inflections that will be used in this book are the scoop, the fall, and the turn.

THE SCOOP:
The scoop is a bend approach before a note. There are a variety of ways to accomplish this. Some musicians adjust their embouchure to lower the pitch of the note while others use their fingers to play a chromatic approach below the note. I recommend thinking of scoops like a chromatic approach. Insert a fast chromatic approach note from below right before the note that you want to play. This avoids many intonation problems that can happen when you change your embouchure and helps develop technique.

This is how a scoop is often notated.

This is how you play it

In this workbook I will always notate scoops as chromatic approach notes!

A scooped scale

Some notes are harder to scoop than others. Focus on scooping whatever notes you find easy on your instrument.

THE FALL:

Falls, which are sometimes called spills or glissandos, are very common inflections that typically occur at the end of phrases. In order to execute a fall you start by playing a note. Once you have played the note that you will to fall from, drastically lower your volume and quickly move in some type of descending pattern. The pattern could be a scale or chromatic scale, but it does not have to be. The further you fall, the softer you get. The loudest note is always the first, not the last.

This is how a typical fall is written.   This is how you play it.

THE TURN:

The turn is another common jazz inflection. To execute a turn, you play a note and then rapidly play the next ascending note, the original note, if time and technique permit the next descending note, before ending on the original note. When turns occur on eighth notes they often just consist of the original note, the next ascending note and a return to the original note.

This is how a turn is written.   This is how you play it.

Turns on a scale.   This is how you play them.

Major Scales

These are the major scales that will be used for the different compositions in this workbook. Make sure you know these scales well. Become proficient at these scales before attempting to play any of the more complicated key signatures in this workbook.

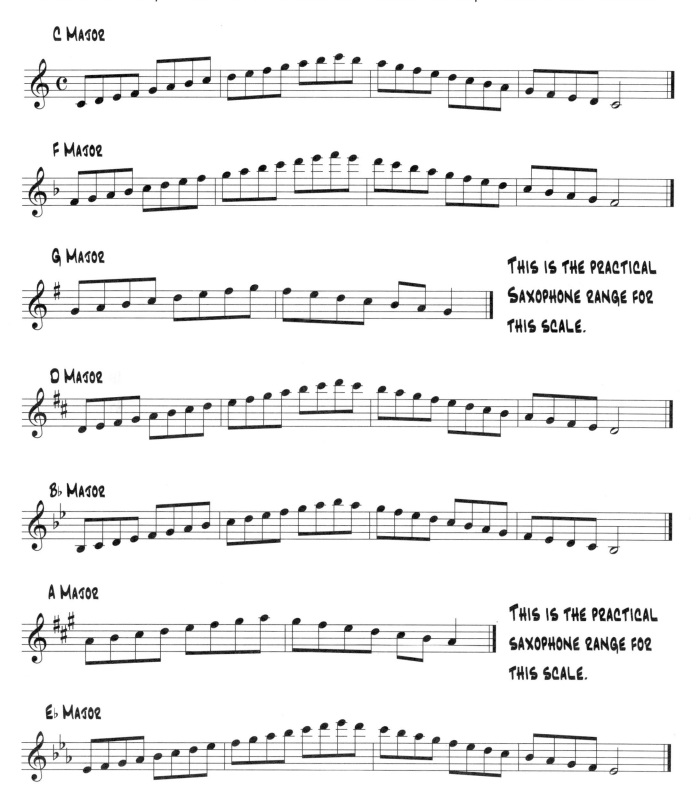

C Major

F Major

G Major

This is the practical saxophone range for this scale.

D Major

Bb Major

A Major

This is the practical saxophone range for this scale.

Eb Major

BLUES SCALES

THESE ARE THE BLUES SCALES THAT MAY BE USED FOR SOME OF THE DIFFERENT COMPOSITIONS IN THIS WORKBOOK. MAKE SURE YOU KNOW THESE SCALES WELL. THE FORMULA FOR CREATING A BLUES SCALE IS LISTED BELOW.

THIS IS THE PRACTICAL SAXOPHONE RANGE FOR THIS SCALE.

THIS IS THE PRACTICAL SAXOPHONE RANGE FOR THIS SCALE.

Swingin' Through The Trees
In "G"

Medium Swing

Once you're comfortable playing this, go to page 59 and try it adding inflections.

Swingin' Through The Trees
in "F"

Medium Swing

Make sure you notate and add your own scoops, turns, and falls to this song.

Swingin' Through The Trees

In "A"

Medium Swing

Make sure you notate and add your own scoops, turns, and falls to this song.

CRAWLIN'
IN "C"

SLOW SWING

ONCE YOU'RE COMFORTABLE PLAYING THIS, GO TO PAGE 60 AND TRY ADDING INFLECTIONS.

Crawlin'
In "F"

Slow Swing

MAKE SURE YOU WRITE IN YOUR OWN SCOOPS, TURNS, AND FALLS TO THIS SONG.

Crawlin'

In "A"

Slow Swing

MAKE SURE YOU WRITE IN YOUR OWN SCOOPS, TURNS, AND FALLS TO THIS SONG.

Struttin'
In "C"

Medium Swing

Make sure you notate and add your own scoops, turns, and falls to this song.

Struttin'
In "D"

Medium Swing

Once you're comfortable playing this, go to page 61 and try adding inflections.

Struttin'
In "Bb"

Medium Swing

Make sure you notate and add your own scoops, turns, and falls to this song.

Right Side Up/ Upside Down
In "C"

Medium Swing

Make sure you write in your own scoops, turns, and falls to this song.

Right Side Up/ Upside Down
In "F"

Medium Swing

When you're comfortable playing this, go to page 62 and try adding inflections.

Right Side Up/ Upside Down
In "A"

Medium Swing

MAKE SURE YOU NOTATE AND ADD YOUR OWN SCOOPS, TURNS, AND FALLS TO THIS SONG.

SMILING BACK
IN "C"

MEDIUM SWING

MAKE SURE YOU NOTATE AND ADD YOUR OWN SCOOPS, TURNS, AND FALLS TO THIS SONG.

Smiling Back
In "G"

Medium Swing

WHEN YOU'RE COMFORTABLE PLAYING THIS, TURN TO PAGE 63 AND TRY ADDING INFLECTIONS.

SMILING BACK
IN "Bb"

Medium Swing

MAKE SURE YOU NOTATE AND ADD YOUR OWN SCOOPS, TURNS, AND FALLS TO THIS SONG.

Stepping Up
In "G"

Medium Swing

Make sure you write in your own scoops, turns, and falls to this song.

Stepping Up
In "Bb"

Medium Swing

Make sure you write in your own scoops, turns, and falls to this song.

Stepping Up
In "A"

Medium Swing

When you're comfortable with this, go to page 64 and try adding inflections.

CRUISIN'
IN "C"

MEDIUM SWING

MAKE SURE YOU NOTATE AND ADD YOUR OWN SCOOPS, TURNS, AND FALLS TO THIS SONG.

CRUISIN'
IN "D"

Medium Swing

Make sure you notate and add your own scoops, turns, and falls to this song.

CRUISIN'
IN "Eb"

MEDIUM SWING

WHEN YOU'RE COMFORTABLE WITH THIS, GO TO PAGE 65 AND TRY ADDING INFLECTIONS.

Blues Ramble
In "C"

Medium Swing

First Ending

Second Ending

Make sure you notate and add your own scoops, turns, and falls to this song.

Blues Ramble
In "G"

Medium Swing

WHEN YOU'RE COMFORTABLE PLAYING THIS, GO TO PAGE 66 AND TRY ADDING INFLECTIONS.

Blues Ramble
In "A"

Medium Swing

Make sure you notate and add your own scoops, turns, and falls to this song.

A Minor Twist
In "C"

Medium Swing

When you're comfortable playing this, go to page 67 and try adding inflections.

A Minor Twist
In "G"

Medium Swing

Make sure you notate and add your own scoops, turns, and falls to this song.

A Minor Twist
In "Bb"

Medium Swing

Make sure you notate and add your own scoops, turns, and falls to this song.

Skippin'
in "C"

Medium Swing

When you're comfortable playing this, go to page 68 and try adding inflections.

Skippin'
in "D"

Medium Swing

MAKE SURE YOU NOTATE AND ADD YOUR OWN SCOOPS, TURNS, AND FALLS TO THIS SONG.

Skippin'

in "E♭"

Medium Swing

MAKE SURE YOU NOTATE AND ADD YOUR OWN SCOOPS, TURNS, AND FALLS TO THIS SONG.

Funky Walk
in "C"

The Eighth Notes in this song are even. Do not swing them!

Slow Funk

Make sure you notate and add your own scoops, turns, and falls to this song.

Funky Walk
in "G"

The Eighth Notes in this song are even. Do not swing them!

Slow Funk

When you're comfortable with this, turn to page 69 and try adding inflections.

Funky Walk

in "A"

The Eighth Notes in this song are even. Do not swing them!

Slow Funk

Make sure you write in your own scoops, turns, and falls to this song.

A Blues Thang
In "G"

Medium Swing

When you're comfortable playing this, go to page 70 and try adding inflections.

A Blues Thang
In "D"

Medium Swing

Make sure you notate and add your own scoops, turns, and falls to this song.

A Blues Thang
In "Eb"

Medium Swing

Make sure you notate and add your own scoops, turns, and falls to this song.

Sneaking About
In "G"

Medium Swing

When you're comfortable with this, turn to page 71 and try adding inflections.

Sneaking About
In "F"

Medium Swing

Make sure you notate and add your own scoops, turns, and falls to this song.

Sneaking About
In "Bb"

Medium Swing

Make sure you notate and add your own scoops, turns, and falls to this song.

Off-Beat Blues
In "C" Blues Scale

Medium Swing

Make sure you notate and add your own scoops, turns, and falls to this song.

Off-Beat Blues
In "G" Blues Scale

Medium Swing

When you're comfortable playing this, turn to page 72 and try adding inflections.

Off-Beat Blues
In "Bb" Blues Scale

Medium Swing

Make sure you write in your own scoops, turns, and falls to this song.

Floating on Up Beats
in "C"

Medium Swing

Make sure you notate and add your own scoops, turns, and falls to this song.

Floating on Up Beats
in "F"

Medium Swing

When you're comfortable with this, turn to page 73 and try adding inflections.

Floating on Up Beats

In "Bb"

Medium Swing

Make sure you notate and add your own scoops, turns, and falls to this song.

Songs with Jazz Inflections

Now we'll look at the same fifteen compositions with jazz inflections written in. Make these inflections a habit! They will make you sound great.

The Scoop

The Turn

The Fall

Swingin' Through The Trees
in "G" With Inflections

Medium Swing

CRAWLIN'
IN "C" WITH INFLECTIONS

MEDIUM SWING

Struttin'

In "D" With Inflections

Slow Swing

Right Side Up/ Upside Down
In "F" With Inflections

Medium Swing

Smiling Back
In "G" with Inflections

Medium Swing

Stepping Up
In "A" with Inflections

Medium Swing

CRUISIN'
IN "E♭" WITH INFLECTIONS

MEDIUM SWING

Blues Ramble
In "G" With Inflections

Medium Swing

First Ending

Second Ending

A Minor Twist

In "C" With Inflections

Medium Swing

Skippin'
in "C" With Inflections

Medium Swing

Funky Walk
in "G" With Inflections

Slow Funk

A Blues Thang
In "G" With Inflections

Medium Swing

Sneaking About
In "G" with Inflections

Medium Swing

Off-Beat Blues
In "G" Blues Scale with Inflections

Medium Swing

Floating on Up Beats
in "F" With Inflections

Medium Swing

About the Author

Brian J. Kane received a B.A. from the Berklee College of Music and an M.S.M. from Bridgewater State College. As a professional saxophonist and flautist, he has performed in over 2000 live performances running the gamut of music styles. As a passionate music educator he has taught classroom music in both public and private schools and given over 10,000 private lessons on saxophone. Brian has developed innovative teaching techniques for jazz styles, sight reading, and melodic improvisational concepts. Presently living in the greater-Boston area, Brian is available for clinics and master classes on a wide variety of topics. For more information or to contact Brian, please visit _www.jazzpath.com_ and click on the Brian Kane link or send inquiries to JazzPath Publishing, PO Box 381810, Cambridge, MA 02238.